Daily Dose

*of Direction for
Women in Business*

Daily Dose
of Direction for Women in Business

A 90 Day Journey to Direct and Guide
Women in Business to Succeed

Melanie Bonita

WINSTON SALEM

DAILY DOSE OF DIRECTION FOR WOMEN IN BUSINESS: A 90 Day Journey to Direct and Guide Women in Business to Succeed

Copyright © 2017 – Melanie Bonita

All rights reserved. This book is protected by the copyright laws of the United States of America. This book may not be copied or reprinted for commercial gain or profit. The use of quotations or occasional page copying for personal or group study is permitted and encouraged. Permission will be granted upon request.

Soft cover ISBN: 978-0-9979923-9-7
eBook ISBN: 978-0-9988313-0-5

Library of Congress Cataloging-in-Publication Data
Names: Bonita, Melanie
Title: Daily dose of direction for women in business/Melanie Bonita;
LCCN: 2017936589
LC record available at https://lccn.loc.gov/2017936589

Melanie Bonita Enterprises
Ormond Beach, FL 32176
www.melaniebonita.com
443-295-3673

Cover design by Chante' Smith of CTS Graphic Designs

Cooke House Publishing
(a division of Cooke Consulting & Creations, LLC)
Winston-Salem, NC
844-287-9364
publishing@cookecc.org

Unless otherwise identified, Scripture quotations are from the King James Version. Copyright © 1982 by Thomas Nelson, Inc. Used by permission. All rights reserved.

Scripture taken from the New King James Version®. Copyright © 1982 by Thomas Nelson. Used by permission. All rights reserved.

Scripture quotations marked (NIV) are taken from the Holy Bible, New International Version®, NIV®. Copyright © 1973, 1978, 1984, 2011 by Biblica, Inc.™ Used by permission of Zondervan. All rights reserved worldwide.

Scripture quotations marked (NLT) are taken from the Holy Bible, New Living Translation, copyright ©1996, 2004, 2007, 2013, 2015 by Tyndale House Foundation. Used by permission of Tyndale House Publishers, Inc., Carol Stream, Illinois 60188. All rights reserved.

Scripture taken from the NEW AMERICAN STANDARD BIBLE®, Copyright © 1960,1962,1963,1968,1971,1972,1973,1975,1977,1995 by The Lockman Foundation. Used by permission.

Scripture quotations taken from the Amplified® Bible (AMP), Copyright © 1954, 1958, 1962, 1964, 1965, 1987 by The Lockman Foundation. Used by permission. www.Lockman.org"

This book and all Cooke House Publishing books are available at Christian bookstores and distributors worldwide.

Printed in the United States of America.- First Edition

This Book is Presented to

_____

By

_____

On the Occasion of

_____

Date

_____

Praise for Daily Dose of Direction for Women in Business

Melanie Bonita is a marketing guru, but most importantly she is a woman of God who shares her blessings and encourages others to so the same.

A *Daily Dose of Direction for Women in Business* is an incredible way to stay focused on the purpose that God has for your life in the business arena. There will always be bumps in the road and even detours but by staying connected to other strong women, you will not lose your way. Thank you Melanie Bonita for bringing together a group of fabulous women to help others stay on track or even find their way.

Dr. Evelyn "Doc" Bethune
Award Winning Author, Lecturer and Motivational Speaker working to expand the knowledge of her grandmother, Dr. Mary McLeod Bethune.

Dedication

This book is dedicated to ALL women in business and women aspiring to start their business. May we know them, may we be them, may we inspire them and support them!

Stay inspired and continue to be the best that God has called you to be.

Acknowledgments

First, I give glory and honor to my Lord and Savior Jesus Christ; He is the head of my life and reason why I do what I do.

To my mother, Lena P. Buckmon, thank you for teaching me how to be self-motivated and about having multiple streams of income.

To my daughter, Crystal L. Buckmon, who brings so much joy to my life.

Thank you to my grandma, Edna March, who went to glory to be with the Lord in December of 2015 at the age of 105. She continued to show and teach me strength in ALL that she did.

To my grandmother, Earline Wright, for introducing me to Jesus Christ at a young age.

To the best pastor in the world, Pastor Michael A. Freeman and his wonderful wife, Dr. DeeDee Freeman, who show me how to live a life of integrity, character, excellence, and how to have a spirit of faith. Much love to the entire Spirit of Faith Christian Center family.

Much love to the Spirit of Faith Bible Institute (SOFBI) and its entire staff.

Thanks to my fabulous celebrity photographer, Jackie Hicks, from Fond Memories Photography. You ALWAYS make me look good. You are the BEST photographer on this side of glory!

Thanks to the amazing Angie BEE who gives her selfless service consistently and made my transition to Florida much more effortlessly easier. The divine connections that you have helped me to make here are priceless. You have one of the biggest hearts and loving spirits.

Thanks to Odessa Hopkins and the Biz Women Online family for creating an awesome online platform for women business owners and entrepreneurs to promote their business. You all are the BEST!

Thanks to Coach Livi Anderson for her dynamic social media training and coaching. My Instagram platform has forever changed as a result of this divine connection with you.

Thanks to Ayanna "Yanni" for ALWAYS reminding me to take care of me, and for your continuous encouragement and support.

Thanks to Dr. Shirley K. Clark of Jabez Books, who continuously gives me speaking engagements and book signing opportunities and supports me in my endeavors.

Thanks to Yvette Munroe and the Holy Millionaire Club members. Your coaching, spiritual insight, and wisdom have tremendously blessed me and my business. Thank you so much for helping me take my business to the next level and showing me what tenacity and bulldog faith look like. I greatly appreciate you and ALL that you do.

Thanks to Anna McCoy. Your encouragement, prayers, and night preaching has changed my life forever. I truly thank God for you and your obedience.

To Theresa R. Proctor, words cannot express how much you have been a blessing to me and my business during this journey. Thank you for your support.

Thanks to Pastor Sarah Morgan, your prayers have truly ignited a fire up under me and have blessed me immensely.

Thanks to the Coleman family who have ALWAYS had my back.

To ALL of my family, friends, and everyone who has ever encouraged, educated, and enlightened me throughout this process: There's no measure that could express my gratitude for how you ALL have helped in my success. May God bless you one thousand–fold Bible return.

Contents

Introduction	20
Women in Business Pray	21
Let the Lord Lead	22
Arise and Shine	23
Ask God	24
Hush vs. Hustle	25
Collaboration Not Competition	26
Above All	27
Just Start	28
Age is Just a Number	29
The Motivational Call	30
Dream Team	31
My Dream Team Is	22
Believe in Your Business	33
Proverbs 31 Business Woman	34
Keep God in It	35
Women in Business Are	36
The Master's Plan	37
Use Your Tax Return	38
Google It	39
Study Your Craft	40
Sow Seeds	41
Use Time Wisely	42
Rest, Relax, & Rejuvenate	43
Work Hard - Play Hard	44
Holistic Health	45
Your Health is Your Wealth	46
Is it a Hobby or a Business?	47
Cash in on Your Passion	48

Daily Deposits	49
What Makes You Rich	50
Multiple Streams of Income	51
No More Freebies	52
Why is it Free?	53
Quality Over Free	54
Drop "Free" From Your Vocabulary	55
Certifications Give Credibility	56
What's in Your Hand?	57
Get Moving with a Mentor	58
Every Coach Needs a Coach	59
Purpose Pusher	60
Walk with the Wise	61
Permission Granted	62
Network Marketing Nuggets	63
Be Your Own Boss	64
Are You Sowing Seeds?	65
Help to Harvest	66
Fulfill a Need	67
From Neo to Pro	68
Caught Between Your Job & Your Dream!	69
We're in this Together	70
Let Love Lead	71
Preparation Brings About a Manifestation	72
Work on Your Masterpiece!	73
As a Woman Thinketh, So is She	74
The Turning Point	75
Freedom to Flow	76
Submission Can Lead You	77
From Employee to Employer	78
Failure is Not an Option	79
Positioned for Success	80

A Quick Work	81
Watchwoman on the Wall	82
Stay in Your Lane	83
Speak it into Existence	84
Watch Your Words	85
The Secret to Success	86
Fall in Love with the Struggle	87
Trials are Only Temporary	88
Be a Better Woman	89
It's Time to Write Your Own Story!	90
Get Your Business in Order	91
Do Your Due Diligence	92
Business and Balance	93
You Got the Power	94
Exude Energy	95
Self-Sabotage	96
The Blame Game	97
Decide to Delegate	98
I Never Thought I Had it in Me!	99
It Takes Faith	100
Our Powerful Purpose	101
No Limits, No Boundaries	102
Prioritizing is the Key	103
God. You. Family. Business. In that Order!	104
Obstacles are Inevitable!	105
Favor with Negotiations	106
Put a Date on It	107
Lean on the Lord	108
Daily Declaration for Women in Business	109
Prayer for Women in Business	110
About the Author	117
Contributing Authors	120

Introduction

This literary work is a compilation of views that will vary. The views, opinions and advice do not necessarily reflect that of the compiler, Melanie Bonita. It is our objective to offer a variety from each author's perspective, experience and wisdom. This strategy alone will offer you the opportunity to personally craft a plan to achieve greater success according to your way of living and how you would like to operate your business.

DAY 1

Women in Business Pray

As a woman in business, it's very important to pray before you start your day. But not only pray before you start your day, but also pray continuously throughout the day and at the end of the day. According to I Thessalonians 5:17 (NKJV), you should *"Pray without ceasing."* Pray to get guidance, wisdom, knowledge and understanding. Spending time in prayer helps you to hear from God. Hearing from God as it relates to your business is essential in increasing your impact, influence, and income. Your business will change as a result of you seeking God through prayer. It's time to go higher in your prayer life and in your business.

Melanie Bonita

DAY 2

Let the Lord Lead

I found that women in business that are led by the Lord can be much more productive, peaceful, and profitable. When we allow the Lord to lead us in our day-to-day activities in our business, we can see greater results much faster. Being led by the Lord allows you to consistently go in the right direction. Psalms 37:23 (NJKV) says, *"The steps of a good man are ordered by the Lord, and He delights in his way."* Ask yourself this question: are you a woman in business who are leading your own way, or are your day-to-day steps being led by the Lord?

Melanie Bonita

DAY 3

Arise and Shine

Arise and Shine, Daughter of Destiny, thine light has come! The old falls off, the new comes upon me. Therefore, I put to death and say backfire to every curse and spirit that limits, delays, and distracts, for life and death is in the power of my tongue. Out of the Womb of the Morning, I declare an open Heaven to new mercies, favor, wisdom, and Glory. God is walled as fire around me and Glory in my midst. Henceforth, goodness and mercy follows and delivers me success. Blessed be my businesses, health, finances, family, and relationships!

Beloved, be encouraged, comforted, and victorious in this, the day of the Lord!

Tracy Horton

DAY 4

Ask God

Instead of telling God what you don't have, start asking God how to get what you need for your business. It doesn't matter what you need. When God gave me the vision for my first book, I had just started work after being laid off for over 5 months. I didn't tell God that I didn't have the money. I asked Him where to get it, and He told me exactly where to get it from. So just do what Matthew 7:7 (NKJV) says, *"Ask, and it will be given to you; seek, and you will find; knock, and it will be opened to you."* It doesn't take much to ask. Just open your mouth.

Melanie Bonita

DAY 5

Hush vs. Hustle

When driven by your passion you can accomplish anything. This is one reason why it's essential that you master listening to your INner voice. There may be times when what you hear doesn't make sense or requires you to change directions midstream. Be cautious not to allow the voice of your hustle to drown out your INner voice. It is in these times you run the risk of being out of alignment with your assignment. Your ability to know when to hush and when to hustle can be the difference between the death and life of your business (*see* Proverbs 8:32-35).

Dawn E. Stephens

DAY 6

Collaboration NOT Competition

A serious woman in business doesn't have time to look around at what others are doing to try to compete with them. We stay focused on making ourselves better and handling our business. We strive to collaborate and work with other powerful women in business. When we support each other the way we should, there really is no time to compete against each other. Our minds should be set on sharpening each other like Proverbs 27:17 (NKJV) shares. It says, *"As iron sharpens iron, So a man sharpens the countenance of his friend."*

Melanie Bonita

DAY 7

Above All

Why are you thinking so small when Ephesians 3:20 (NKJV) says, *"Now to Him who is able to do exceedingly abundantly above all that we ask or think, according to the power that works in us."* So, if you think about the words "above all," what is it above all that you've been thinking you want? Well, I can tell you right now that you've already been thinking too small if you're not thinking above all. It's time to stop your stinking thinking and start thinking like what Jesus said that He would give you, and that is "above all." Let's stop thinking so small and let's do it much bigger because He said "above all"!

Melanie Bonita

DAY 8

Just Start

Don't stay stagnant when you're thinking about what is needed to start your business. You might be thinking that you need a logo, a website, flyers, and other business materials. Well, I'm here to tell you that it doesn't have to cost a lot to get those things. What if I told you that you could literally get a professional logo, book cover, website, and/or just about ANYTHING that you need for your business for ONLY $5? Yes, it's true. So just go ahead and get started and go over to fiverr.com to make it happen. Don't think about how much it's going to cost or how much time it's going to take! JUST START!

Melanie Bonita

DAY 9

Age Is Just a Number

You are never too young or too old to start or work on your business. Have you heard about the 9-year-old girl that received a million-dollar contract with a national health food chain for her lemonade? You may have started a business or book years ago but quit too soon. You're not too old to go back to it. I know a gentleman who wrote his first book at age 101. Remember the stories of Joseph and Kind David from the Bible. David was the youngest of his brothers, but God still used him in a mighty way. Joseph was close to the youngest. They both reigned and ruled. I just love what Jeremiah 1:7 (NLT) says: *"The Lord replied, "Don't say, 'I'm too young,' for you must go wherever I send you and say whatever I tell you.""*

Melanie Bonita

DAY 10

The Motivational Call

I don't have lots of time for idle chit chat, but some calls stop me in my tracks. These calls involve laughing and learning. They are what I refer to as Motivational Calls. They're unexpected and unrehearsed but beneficial to both parties. That's what makes them worthwhile.

Entrepreneurs work tirelessly on their mission sometimes with little interaction. So, motivational calls are life's way of saying, "STOP whatever you're doing and breathe." And, it's the caller's way of saying, "You're busy but this is what you need." And…it usually is.

Your next motivational call might be from me, so remember to pick up!

Odessa Hopkins

DAY 11

Dream Team

It takes a team to effectively carry out the vision that God has placed within you. You may want to, but you can't do it all by yourself. Pray and ask God to send you your dream team. Your dream team will have a passion for your vision and will want to help you with it. Even Jesus had a dream team. The twelve disciples helped carry out the vision and mission of saving the lost. They left everything they had to be a part of Jesus' team. Look what Luke 18:28 (NIV) says about it: *"Peter said to him, "We have left all we had to follow you!"*

Melanie Bonita

DAY 12

My Dream Team Is...

Dedicated and Driven

Ready and Reliable

Essential and Enthusiastic

Attentive and Able

Mission-minded and Motivated

Timely and Teachable

Equipped and Effective

Ambitious and Anticipating the Need

Mindful and Moving Forward

Melanie Bonita

DAY 13

Believe in Your Business

When you believe in God and believe in your business, NOTHING will be impossible for you! There's a shift that takes place when you believe. There's a level of confidence that exudes when you believe in your business. When you believe and exercise your faith, you will start taking the necessary actions to increase your business. Check out Matthew 17:20 (NKJV). It says, *"So Jesus said to them, "Because of your unbelief; for assuredly, I say to you, if you have faith as a mustard seed, you will say to this mountain, 'Move from here to there,' and it will move; and nothing will be impossible for you."* It's your belief that makes the difference!

Melanie Bonita

DAY 14

Proverbs 31 Business Woman

Proverbs 31 reflection of a business woman is to provide peace from a unique perspective to bless all mankind.

God purposefully and divinely created women for entrepreneurship. He gifted every woman with a natural ability to serve. Commissioned out of the ribs of a man, God promises to bless woman beyond the fruit of her labor.

Women in business bridge the gaps during complex and competitive situations where only strongholds can be released through strategic and organized planning. Through strong leadership, positive thinking, and loyalty, God blesses women entrepreneurs with a Deuteronomy 28 overflow.

Deuteronomy 28: 11 (KJV) says, *"And the Lord shall make thee plenteous in goods, in the fruit of thy body, and in the fruit of thy cattle, and in the fruit of thy ground, in the land which the Lord sware unto thy fathers to give thee."*

Orjanette Bryant

DAY 15

Keep God in It

First, I applaud you! You're taking steps to become a SUCCESSFUL business woman.

Dream big and never let anyone tell you it's impossible.

It starts with a vision from God but IMPLEMENTATION is key.

Faith in God AND determination are required to achieve your dreams.

Step outside your comfort zone. God will use you in unimaginable ways.

I'm an unconventional success story. All I know is that God has blessed me and I give Him honor and thanks for all that He's done and continues to do in my personal and professional life.

Jaclyn Gary

DAY 16

Women in Business Are:

Willing to Work
Optimistic
Motivated
Ethical
Noble

Integral
Negotiator

Builder
Unique
Successful
Innovative
Necessary
Enthusiastic
Supportive
Strong

Melanie Bonita

DAY 17

The Master's Plan

Many times you take time out to schedule your daily, weekly, monthly and/or annual plan for your business. It's great to plan, but be open to shift when or if God changes your plans. His plans are so much better than yours. You may think you have put together the perfect plan, but believe me, when you carry out God's plan for your business, it is so much better. Consider Jeremiah 29:11. It says, *"For I know the plans I have for you," declares the Lord, "plans to prosper you and not to harm you, plans to give you hope and a future."* All of His plans are designed to work for your good. The only way it won't work is if you deviate from His plan and try to work your own plan.

Melanie Bonita

DAY 18

Use Your Tax Return

When people used to tell me that they didn't have enough money to start their business, I would share my testimony with them of how I got the money to publish my first book. I remember asking God where I was going to get the resources necessary to publish it. He reminded me that I hadn't filed my tax returns yet. After I filed them, I realized that it was one of the biggest tax returns that I had ever received. You see, the money was already there. I just had to ask and do the work to make it available. Matthew 7:7 (NKJV) makes it clear for us to *"Ask and it will be given to you; seek and you will find; knock and the door will be opened to you."*

Melanie Bonita

DAY 19

Google It

Times have changed drastically and technology has changed with time. Because of technology, you have so many resources right at your fingertips. There is no reason for not being able to find the information that you're looking for. All you have to do now is "Google It!" Long gone are the days where you have to look in an encyclopedia. Most youth don't even know what an encyclopedia is now. Stop trying to guess and figure it out on your own. Just "Google It!" Google also owns YouTube now. YouTube has a plethora of videos that will show you how to do just about anything for your business. So, get on your computer, tablet, or phone and make it happen.

Melanie Bonita

DAY 20

Study Your Craft

Whatever your business or whatever you're working on, you should be the best at it. You should be known as the subject matter expert (SME) in your field. Some may call it the "go to" person. In order to become the SME, you must know what you are doing. You must study your craft. Studies show that if you spend 10,000 hours studying a subject you have mastered it. II Timothy 2:15 (KJV) says, *"Study to shew thyself approved unto God, a workman that needeth not be ashamed, rightly dividing the word of truth."* There are books to read and trainings to attend to learn more about your business. Take time out and spend time studying so that you can enhance what you already know.

Melanie Bonita

DAY 21

Sow Seeds

In your daily activities, you should be sowing several seeds into your business. In this case, I'm talking about making new contacts, sharing your business, and activities that will help you reach more people to grow your business. In one business that I was part of, we called it the "10 a day" rule. That means you didn't go home until you had shared your business with at least 10 new people each day. Try doing this in your business for at least 30 days, and watch the harvest that you reap from the seeds you have sown. If you sow the right seeds in the right ground, in due season, you shall surely reap a harvest.

Melanie Bonita

DAY 22

Use Time Wisely

Everyone has the same 24 hours in a day. Why is it that some people are much more productive than others? Are the unproductive people spending time doing things that don't contribute to their dreams? When people tell me that they don't have time to work on their business or write their book, I ask them how much time do they spend watching television or surfing social media? Think about what YOU can change in your schedule so that you can use your time more wisely.

Melanie Bonita

DAY 23

Rest, Relax & Rejuvenate

As business women, we want to grind, hustle, and handle our business. Even in all of that, we must make time to rest, relax, and rejuvenate at least once a week. Even the Lord rested after He worked. Exodus 20:11 (NKJV) says, *"For in six days the Lord made the heavens and the earth, the sea, and all that is in them, and rested the seventh day."* Resting is essential in order for us to live the abundant life that God has called us to live. Going to the spa and getting a massage is a great way to relax and rejuvenate. Do something special after a long week's work. Your body and mind will love you for it!

Melanie Bonita

DAY 24

Work Hard - Play Hard

Just because you have your own business, it doesn't mean that you can't enjoy life and have fun. Yes, many entrepreneurs work harder than most people that work a traditional job, especially in the beginning years. Since you work hard, you should play just as hard. Ask God for strategies and systems that you can put into place so that you can work smarter instead of harder to get the same or even better results. Reward yourself for your work and completed tasks. Travel the world and spend more time with your family and doing what you really enjoy.

Melanie Bonita

DAY 25

Holistic Health

I'm finding that way too many women have not been productive or are unable to work on their business because of health challenges. I declare and decree that your health challenges are over in Jesus' Name. He said in His word, *"Beloved, I pray that in every way you may succeed and prosper and be in good health [physically], just as [I know] your soul prospers [spiritually]."* III John 2 (AMP). So because His word says that, then we need to believe it. I encourage you—every time you receive a diagnosis or encounter a health challenge, to find out what the holistic natural remedy or solution for it is, so that you can be healthy and whole to do the work that God has called you to do.

Melanie Bonita

DAY 26

Your Health Is Your Wealth

What is wealth if you don't have your health? Even having money and all the stuff that goes along with it is nothing if you don't have good health. If you are not healthy, you won't be able to thoroughly enjoy the wealth and riches that you may have. That's why it is imperative that you take care of the temple (body) that God has blessed you with. If you really think about it, your body doesn't even belong to you. In I Corinthians 6:19 (NIV), it says, *"Do you not know that your bodies are temples of the Holy Spirit, who is in you, whom you have received from God? You are not your own."* Therefore, we should eat right, exercise, and do everything we can to take great care of our temple.

Melanie Bonita

DAY 27

Is It a Hobby or a Business?

Do you feel like you're not earning enough income in your business? Do you feel like your business is not growing the way you would like it to or as fast as you would like it to? Are you really putting in the work it takes to effectively and efficiently run your business? Well, if you treat your business like a hobby, it will pay you like a hobby; but if you treat your business like a business, it will pay you like a business. You need to put in the time and effort to get the real results from your business.

Melanie Bonita

DAY 28

Cash In on Your Passion

Why are you spending so much time doing what you don't enjoy when you can get paid to do what you love? There are so many ways that you can cash in on your passion and make lots of money doing what you're passionate about. Proverbs 18:6 (NKJV) says, *"A man's gift makes room for him, And brings him before great men."* You might have to be creative to turn your passion and gifts into a business. You can go to trainings and also read books to learn how to make that happen. Discover essential habits that business owners have. You also should invest in the proper tools. Know that it's possible.

Melanie Bonita

DAY 29

Daily Deposits

I declare and decree daily deposits from your business into your bank accounts, PayPal accounts, Square accounts, shopping carts, and any other payment method that you have. People are purchasing your products and/or services daily, day and night, even while you are asleep. Your accounts are overflowing as a result of these daily deposits. Job 22:28 (NKJV) says, *"You will also declare a thing, And it will be established for you; So light will shine on your ways."* And so shall it be in Jesus' Name!

Melanie Bonita

DAY 30

What Makes You Rich

According to Proverbs 10:4 (NKJV), *"He who has a slack hand becomes poor, But the hand of the diligent makes rich."* It's time to really get diligent in working your business so that you can get rich. In one of the businesses I was part of, we used to say take massive action to get that money. God wants you rich, but you have to do the work to get there because faith without works is dead. Some of you are hoping, wishing, and praying that your business would grow and expand. There's nothing wrong with praying that your business would grow, but you must be diligent in doing the work too.

Melanie Bonita

DAY 31

Multiple Streams of Income

It is said that the average millionaire has at least 7 streams of income. How many streams of income do you have? If you only have one stream of income, what would happen if you lose that one? You can easily add something on the side or something additional to compliment your current business to add more streams of income. After the first time that I was laid off from a job, I realized the importance of having more than one stream of income. Ask God what you can do to add additional streams to your income so that the flow will never run dry.

Melanie Bonita

DAY 32

NO More Freebies!

I used to think that I needed to do freebies to "attract" clients.

- This Instagram Expert has 2 free programs
- Oohh... That one has a free class. Maybe I should do that too...

Then it hit me:

Why do you need to do anything for free if you have RESULTS and people can see that you have what they need??? I didn't get to 140,000 Instagram followers for free. I invested, gained wisdom, and shifted from flopping around at 60,000 followers with no strategy to standing as an expert 80,000 followers and dozens of clients later.

Livi Anderson

DAY 33

Why is it FREE?

1. If they want it for free then they aren't ready to launch a profitable business.

2. No one is walking around asking for free laundry detergent to wash clothes. Why do you feel the need to give free advice to those who are starting out in your industry?

3. There is enough FREE content posted on the Internet all day, everyday, 365 days a year.

4. There are people who value you, including your tribe and your soul mate clients who will love and respect you too much to EVER try to take advantage of you.

Livi Anderson

DAY 34

Quality Over FREE

I got over FREE very quickly when I realized that quality clients are NEVER looking for a handout. They don't want to just PICK YOUR BRAIN.

Quality clients are looking for a book, an eCourse, an event, a strategy guide, or a private consultation. They are hungry and they are resourceful.

If they don't have the money they will find ways to obtain the money to get what they need.

You will stop desperately searching for the next client and you will pour out of love for your business. The pouring will attract. The love will connect. The wisdom will be clear and the QUALITY clients will take action.

Livi Anderson

DAY 35

Drop "FREE" From Your Vocabulary!

When you stop comparing yourself to every other "xxx expert" in your field you will quickly lose the need to do anything for FREE.

Show up. Build relationships. Then make the offer (aka SELL).

You have permission to push the envelope.

You have authority to move beyond fear.

You have the right to stand up and stand out.

Last but not least, you have the responsibility to drop free from your vocabulary.

Livi Anderson

DAY 36

Certifications Gives Credibility

Do you want more credibility in your business? Then get some certifications. Do certifications really make a difference? Absolutely! It could mean the difference in winning a million-dollar contract. If you're looking to win government contracts, having an 8a, WBE, and/or Veterans Owned certification, will give your business priority over businesses that have no certification. As a woman in business, at a minimum you should be a certified Women Owned Business. Let's make getting certified a priority so that you and your business are a priority!

Melanie Bonita

DAY 37

What's in Your Hand?

There are going to be times in your business when you are just going to have to use what you already have to get what you want or need. You may want the newest equipment, but it might not be in your business budget. Ask God what you already have in your business, in your hand, or home that you can use. The widow woman thought she only had a jar of oil. But the man of God showed her what to do with it. II Kings 4:2 (NKJV) says, *"So Elisha said to her, "What shall I do for you? Tell me, what do you have in the house?" And she said, "Your maidservant has nothing in the house but a jar of oil."* Please read the entire chapter to get the full story.

Melanie Bonita

DAY 38

Get Moving With a Mentor

It is imperative that as a business woman you have a mentor. Having a mentor that has already accomplished what you want to do, can help minimize or eliminate your learning curve. The Bible says to get counsel. Proverbs 11:14 (NKJV) says, *"Where there is no counsel, the people fall; But in the multitude of counselors there is safety."* Why reinvent the wheel when a mentor already has the answers? If you don't have one, get out there and ask. You need several mentors for different areas of your business so that you can get your business moving fast forward.

Melanie Bonita

DAY 39

Every Coach Needs a Coach

In addition to a mentor, you also need a coach. Even if you're already a coach and you coach others, you still need a coach to help lead and guide you. You don't know everything there is to know about coaching others. A coach is different than a mentor. A coach is more hands on, actually coaching you through the process. We should always be in learning mode. In the Bible, Timothy had Paul and there are many more examples too. When you have a coach, please remember to remain coachable to get the maximum benefits.

Melanie Bonita

DAY 40

Purpose Pusher

My personal motto is, "If you don't want me to push you to your next level of success, please don't share your dreams with me." I love being a midwife to women who want to live purpose-filled lives. As a mother of two boys, I know all too well that exertion and birthing go hand in hand. Nothing just happens. Today is your day to push. It is time for God's purpose for your life and business to emerge. Your prayer should be, Lord, give me the strength and courage to give birth to every seed you have planted inside me. In Jesus' Name, amen.

Lady Bobette Brown

DAY 41

Walk With the Wise

It only takes one person to help you catapult your business to the next dimension. It's time for you to start walking with people that are wiser than you so that you can really go to the next dimension. You should never be the smartest person in your circle. That wiser person can give you one idea or one nugget that can translate financially to thousands or even millions. Check out this scripture that talks about walking with the wise: *"Walk with the wise and become wise; associate with fools and get in trouble."* Proverbs 13:20 (NLT). So, start making those divine connections with others that are wiser than you.

Melanie Bonita

DAY 42

Permission Granted

Sister, take back YOUR life and finally focus on YOUR dreams! As you begin this journey, give yourself permission to STAY (Start Thinking About You).

Here are 3 action items to help you embrace S.T.A.Y.

- ✓ <u>Get a Mentor</u> – Be strategic. This person should be someone who has successfully done what you aspire to do.

- ✓ <u>Unsubscribe- Just Say NO</u> – You cannot say YES to everything. You do not have to always explain your NO.

- ✓ <u>Push Pause Daily</u> – Daily carve time out for YOU. Take a walk, read, exercise, journal, spend time in devotion, be still.

Kelli Y. Stonework

Aileen,
Give yourself permission to S.T.A.Y.
Be Blessed
Kelli

DAY 43

Network Marketing Nuggets

If you want to start a business but don't know how or where to start, you are not alone. The best thing to do is network with others. It's best to create work you love, something you would do for free. Remember, everything and anything can be sold. Find someone else that is very successful at selling the product you are interested in and copy, copy, copy. There's nothing wrong with that in business. I am a single mom and I love talking to people of all walks of life. I have sold almost everything from healthy coffee to baby blankets. Just make sure there is always a profit to be made.

Stacey L. Florio

DAY 44

Be Your Own Boss

It's a wonderful thing owning your own business and being your own boss. The end-of-the-year tax benefits are even better. In my business, we have inspirational sayings to keep us going like S.W.S.W.S.W.S.W.N. which stands for SOME WILL, SOME WON'T, SO WHAT, SO WHO'S NEXT? Essentially this means that you don't let one customer upset you. Don't allow any one person to destroy your whole world and set you back. You must keep moving. Don't make time for them in your world. And remember: IF IT IS TO BE IT IS UP TO ME. ALWAYS PUT GOD FIRST IN WHATEVER YOU DO AND YOU WILL NEVER FAIL.

Stacey L. Florio

DAY 45

Are You Sowing Seeds?

Are you sowing seeds? Are you mentoring? Volunteering? Do you have some elderly neighbors that you could help? Is there a community center in your neighborhood or perhaps a local school that could use your services or talents? Look for ways to give back unselfishly and without regard to monetary gain. You will be surprised at the blessings that begin to flow from heaven.

Hebrews 6:10 (NIV) says: *"God is not unjust; He will not forget your work and the love you have shown Him as you have helped His people and continue to help them."*

Lillie West

DAY 46

Help to Harvest

My pastor made an interesting statement in a sermon one day. He said, "If you're finding that you are not reaching your goals and dreams perhaps it is because you are not serving others."

You must sow in order to reap, for without sowing the seeds there is no harvest to reap. We all have the capability to add value to another person's life.

Lillie West

DAY 47

Fulfill a Need

Jesus saw a need, He felt something about it, and then He acted on what he saw.

*Acknowledge that you see the need

*Accept that you feel something about the need

*Act on the need

Learning to serve those who can't pay or repay can be very powerful. It will supply the answer to meet someone's need and you will also discover that it will fulfill a need for you as well.

Lillie West

DAY 48

From Neo to Pro

*Find someone to share your wins with!

*Correspond with those who reach out to you. Everyone will not wait.

*Breathe. Things will get difficult and stressful. Don't panic. Breathe. Think clearly and work through it. Come back to it later, if possible.

*Make Money!

*Take responsibility for the good and the bad. Your character is on display.

*It's not always that they don't believe in you nor support you. Sometimes they want to see consistency or the fruit (outcome, results). For those who display support, be certain to express your gratitude.

*Sow

Newsflash! People are watching! Connect with me because #VisibilityMatters!

Toya Hamlett

DAY 49

Caught Between Your Job & Your Dream!

You know what you want to do!

You know what you want to be!

Due to responsibilities

Finances have become a major priority.

Yet, you believe! There is a way to fit in the two!

Yes, there is a purpose for your job!

Embrace opportunities to use your gifts,

So life won't feel ordinary and odd!

Balancing your job, doing your passion,

Has helped you become an excellent time manager!

Wisdom and Humility are the keys God gives to you

To help you shift from your job to

Your dream!

Ayana "Yanni" Bernard

DAY 50

We're in This Together

In a world that is sometimes filled with a requirement that we all "feel good" and we search for instant gratification, sometimes it is necessary for us to just feel the sadness of life gone too soon, unrealized dreams, and lost love. It is okay to just mourn for a time and allow that sadness to connect us to the humanity that has no color, race, or creed; no political designations or levels of class; just the connection of our human selves. It is evident that all too often we forget that we are all in this human experience together, finding it all too easy to be disrespectful, hate-filled, and on the extreme, murderous.

Dr. Evelyn Bethune

DAY 51

Let Love Lead

In the midst of our identity struggles we must always remember to love first. No, it is not easy, but it is necessary. Remembering to love does not mean that we ignore hateful behavior or fall silent in the face of taking a responsible position in the pursuit of freedom. It is because of love that we must stand up for righteousness and truth. We must take a position and not be afraid to defend it, putting God first and always dealing with issues based on godly principles. Kindness but an expectation of excellence, compassion but insistence on learning to "fish" not just waiting to be given a fish, and an attitude of gratitude will help to build a foundation that can support reclamation and revitalization of the human spirit.

Dr. Evelyn Bethune

DAY 52

Preparation Brings About a Manifestation

In 2000, we established our Writer's Agency. I wasn't sure how to do it or what to do, but I kept hearing these words in my spirit, "Preparation brings about a manifestation." It was after I created the brochure, a website, and business card that people began to call and ask me about publishing a book. Ecclesiastes 11:4 (TLB) says, *"If you wait for perfect conditions, you will never get anything done."* Throughout my life, many people wanted to do what I am doing. Well, in actuality, anyone can do what I am doing per se. They just have to prepare for it. There is no right time really as it is being rightly prepared. If you want to start a business, prepare for it. You have to move from hoping and praying to praying and preparing, and the manifestation will come.

Dr. Shirley K. Clark

DAY 53

Work on Your Masterpiece!

So often we encounter things that challenge our dreams or we hear the internal GPS say again "rerouting." We get discouraged, frustrated, and thoughts of quitting arise. Life happens but it doesn't have to change the dream. Have you ever watched any of the shows on HGTV? They come into a house where all hope is gone and upon completion it's a masterpiece. Sometimes our dreams look just like that, hopeless. Don't quit; go back to blueprint. If the plan isn't working, don't change the dream, change the plan. Life will give you twist and turns, but you must remain focused and keep moving. Remember, you are working on a masterpiece!

Dr. Kelley Perry

DAY 54

As a Woman Thinketh, So Is She

"We are prone to believe more than what we see… What we believe determines what we shall see… More defeats and failures are due to mental blindness than to moral deviations."
- Dr. Raymond Holliwell

Earlier on life's journey, I misplaced the key to unlock my dreams. It is the substance of faith; unwavering belief. Gifts wrapped as lessons taught me to keep centered on faith in all things. I learned that in order to thrive, you have to focalize your dreams, yet remain adaptable. Living abundantly demands courageously declaring audacious dreams and evolving into women who deserve what we thirst for. Contemplating business objectives? Set mammoth intentions. Decide who you'll become, divorce what doesn't serve you (mindset, destructive language, procrastination), then win!

Camille A. John

DAY 55

The Turning Point

Have you ever read a book that started out real slow and just when you're about to give up on reading it something juicy happens and you can't put it down? Life is the same way. Sometimes it starts out slow and right when you're ready to throw in the towel, a real good turning point comes along and changes your whole course. I encourage you today, before you give up on your business, hopes, dreams, and relationships, remember every good book has a turning point. Wait in expectancy for your moment and seize it; you can still finish strong.

T. Lynn Tate

DAY 56

Freedom to Flow

Every seed of guilt planted in your life expires now. I declare you will receive a dose of liberation today. Your life assignment requires dimensions of freedom to flow in business and family. Proverbs 14:1 says, *"Every wise woman buildeth her house."* Balance is nonexistent. It implies every compartment of your life will receive equal attention. The application of wisdom will deliver congruity to each area of your life. This denotes all areas of your life will receive its required attention and time. Great service starts at home. You possess the authority to experience magnificence at the office and at home.

Theresa R. Proctor

DAY 57

Submission Can Lead You

Relationships and entrepreneurship can be challenging for some folks; there can be fear, angst, and trepidation. Painful pasts can cause you to be domineering! So, what do you do when the voice of God tells you to "submit"? Here's my story:

When God guided Bartee to find me, I was angry, unforgiving, and questionable. "God, what am I supposed to do with HIM?!" His answer? "Submit." Job 22:21 says, *"Yield now and be at peace with Him; Thereby good will come to you."* My husband is now my business partner and we've grown closer to the Lord - together. SUBMIT!

Evangelist Angie BEE

DAY 58

From Employee to Employer

I never thought like an employee. I always envisioned myself doing something greater. In December of 2011 when the opportunity presented itself, I decided to "step out on faith" which coincidentally was the title of a sermon at my church six months earlier. I had a job earning a six-figure salary, but I was an employee. I made decisions that had to be approved or commissioned by someone in authority. The day when an employee realizes they are not that person, becomes the day that the employee should envision becoming the employer. Planning for my transition from employee to employer did not come without growing pains but it was worth it.

Sylvia L. Johnson

DAY 59

Failure Is Not An Option

Being an employer would mean leaving the security of a decent salary and benefits and a life style that was comfortable. But being an employee also meant that I was vulnerable to the whims of my employer – downsizing, mergers and acquisitions, and performance metrics. I witnessed first-hand other directors in fear of being laid off. I knew the collective expectations would carry over into my own business and I would be accountable for my success or my failure. I also knew that I was venturing into a male dominated industry that did not overwhelmingly accept women in decision-making roles. At that moment, I proclaimed that failure is not an option.

Sylvia L. Johnson

DAY 60

Positioned For Success

Since the inception of my company, we faced some uphill battles, but I continually positioned myself for success. With business certifications, strategic partnerships, mentors, teaming arrangements, listening to real thinkers, and continual learning, I know that my decision has positively changed my life. Today, we are a successful Health Information Technology/Biomedical Consulting Company with clients spanning the globe. Every morning I start my day by thanking God for His grace and mercy along with people who sacrificed, trusted, and believed in my vision, even with all of the bumps, while repeating my affirmation that failure is not an option.

Sylvia L. Johnson

DAY 61

A Quick Work

When people tell you that it won't happen overnight, that it's a process, or that it might take a while because Rome wasn't built over night, tell them that your Bible says in Amos 9:13 (MSG) *"Yes indeed, it won't be long now." God's decree."* Things are going to happen so fast your head will swim, one thing fast on the heels of the other. You won't be able to keep up. Everything will be happening at once—and everywhere you look, blessings!" Your business is based on the word of God, not what they say. Remind them that God can do a quick work.

Melanie Bonita

DAY 62

Watchwoman on the Wall

The Women's Liberation Movement has opened doors for us. If you are a working wife or a working mother, your home is priority and is a ministry. My mother worked but she never neglected the home. Proverbs 31:11 says, *"The heart of her husband safely trusts her."* Proverbs 31:28 says, *"Her children rise up and call her blessed."* Don't forsake your assignment to conform to the world's standards. Proverbs 31:27 states, *"She watches over the ways of her household."* You are the watchwoman on the wall. You have ownership, an invested interest in the home. Remember, Satan does not take vacations.

Regina Nunnally

DAY 63

Stay In Your Lane

I see way too many women in business comparing themselves to other women in business, then try to be like them. Stop looking around to see what everyone else is doing. God specifically created and designed you for a special assignment and purpose. Don't copy what others are doing. Stay in your lane and do what God has called you to do. You will see many ideas and may even think that you can do better than another, but I encourage you to stay focused on what God has anointed YOU to do.

Melanie Bonita

DAY 64

Speak It Into Existence

What is it that you REALLY want in your life and in your business? Seriously speaking… What is it that you REALLY, REALLY, REALLY want? Are you speaking it into existence? Are you saying DAILY affirmations so that you can obtain what you want, need, and desire? Well I'm here to tell you that if you do what Romans 4:17 (NKJV) says, you can have what you want. It says, *"Call those things which do not exist as though they did."* If you really believe that, you would speak more over your life. Start speaking DAILY over your business, dreams, and aspirations. EVERYTHING you believe God for can be brought forth, out of your mouth. Speak it forth NOW, in Jesus' Name!

Melanie Bonita

DAY 65

Watch Your Words

Do you know how powerful your words are? You better watch what you say out of your mouth. We've heard so many things from our childhood that may not have lined up with God's Word. I know it takes a lot of retraining. But make a decision to change your vocabulary and say what the Word says. Then watch the changes take place in your life and in your business. When you speak negative things about your business, they come to pass too. That's why you really have to watch what you say. Proverbs 18:21 (NKJV) says, *"Death and life are in the power of the tongue, And those who love it will eat its fruit."* It's not just the good that you say, it's the bad too.

Melanie Bonita

DAY 66

The Secret to Success

Many people want to know what the secret to success is, but they never refer to the Bible to find it. ALL of the answers to everything we need are found in the Bible; even the answers to our business ventures. Joshua 1:8 (NKJV) gives us the secret. It says, *"This Book of the Law shall not depart from your mouth, but you shall meditate in it day and night, that you may observe to do according to all that is written in it. For then you will make your way prosperous, and then you will have good success."* Not only will you have success, but it will be good success. It's no longer a secret. You have the answer now. So go do it!

Melanie Bonita

DAY 67

Fall in Love with the Struggle

Wisdom, power, and growth are born in the struggle. As entrepreneurs, the struggle is where the answers are found, where adventure lies, and where we learn to fight for our dreams.

Challenges hone our skills, force us to grow into the identity of who we want to be, and make us strong. The moment you think you're ready to quit is the moment right before a miracle happens.

"For I consider that the sufferings of this present time are not worthy to be compared with the glory which shall be revealed in us" (Romans 8:18 NKJV).

Kelly Campbell

DAY 68

Trials Are Only Temporary

If you're going through a trial in your life or business right now, KNOW that it is only temporary! KNOW that things are going to change very soon in your life. Make sure that you take the necessary actions to help them to change. There may be someone that you know that have gone through a similar trial. Ask them what they did to get out of it and turn that situation around. Remember that II Corinthians 4:17 (NLT) says, *"For our present troubles are small and won't last very long."* Once that trial is over, your business can explode the way you want it to.

Melanie Bonita

DAY 69

Be A Better Woman

One of my biggest pet peeves for women in business is to over commit then under deliver. It is important to only promise what you know you can perform. It is better to over deliver and it be a surprise than to exaggerate your capacity thus compromising your results. Loyalty is birthed from integrity! Commit to quality, excellence and #SoulWealth which is abundance, compassion, and authenticity in every area of your life. Once you vow to be a BETTER WOMAN, your business will testify of your character and your company and brand will reap the benefits.

Elder Vikki Johnson

DAY 70

It's Time to Write Your Own Story!

People love categories because they help process information and simplify the world. We classify everything from foods and animals to cars and buildings. But, let's be honest. Our favorite pastime is labeling people. Intelligent and rich are descriptors that many would love. What about lazy and dumb?

The problem with labels is they reinforce how the giver sees you and also shape how you see yourself. Why give someone the power to define who you are? Considered a "numbers person" but ready to express your creative side? Used to being behind the scenes but want a starring role? Then, erase that label, and write your own story!

Shonette Charles

DAY 71

Get Your Business in Order

God is a God of order, so in order for your business to flourish, you've got to get your business in order. Stop just doing things haphazardly with no order. I Corinthians 14:20 (NKJV) says, *"Let all things be done decently and in order."* If you need help, have someone come in and help you get organized. Whatever you do, don't make excuses for your disorder. That is NOT of God. While working on bringing things in order, make small daily steps and changes, because if you try to do too much at one time, it can become overwhelming. Once you start getting your business in order, you will start to see the good changes in other areas of your business.

Melanie Bonita

DAY 72

Do Your Due Diligence

Woman of God, in business it is imperative to do your due diligence. If you are going to use a company to do services for you or outsource them to your clients, you should thoroughly do your research to make sure that they actually "do" what they say that they are going to do. I've found out that getting testimonials are a great way to confirm. I also like to talk to clients that have used them before. Before you purchase that new office equipment, check out the reviews. There are many ways that you can do your due diligence. Doing it can save you time, energy, and money in the long run.

Melanie Bonita

DAY 73

Business and Balance

Balance is not found, it is created. Everything in life is about balance, even more so when you are a mother and business woman. One of the most important things as a business woman is to have balance. Creating balance is as unique as your finger print. What works for you might not work for others. Make time for God, yourself, family, and business. As an entrepreneur, sometimes work becomes our entire life. But there comes a season were everything must stop and the focus needs to be on personal and spiritual growth to recharge. Then get back to business.

Tiffany Marshall

DAY 74

You Got the Power

Deuteronomy 8:18 (NKJV) says, "*And you shall remember the LORD your God, for it is He who gives you power to get wealth, that He may establish His covenant which He swore to your fathers, as it is this day.*" So now you know that you have the power to get wealthy. It's ALREADY within you. You just need to walk in that power that God has given you. It's time for you to use that power and the ability that He has already given you to produce the wealth that He has called you to have. When you really understand the power that you have, you will never walk in lack again.

Melanie Bonita

DAY 75

Exude Energy

There are going to be times in a day when you feel tired, drained, worn out, or burnt out. But I guarantee you, if you always exude energy and be enthusiastic when you're conducting business, that will rub off on others. Whatever is on you tends to rub off on the person that you're talking to or connected to. Have you ever walked by someone and they were looking down? Then you smiled and they smiled back. It's because whatever is on you had to exude on them too. So, it's time out for just being sad and down and out. Great energy can affect your business. People always say that they just love my energy. What does your energy look like?

Melanie Bonita

DAY 76

Self-Sabotage

Sometimes people feel like the world around us gets hard and things are attacking us. People even blame it on the enemy, when it might just be the inner me. There are times when you might find it hard to move forward or go further in business because of situations and circumstances around you. The truth is, many times it's self-sabotage. It's the things you say to yourself, the things that you think, and the things that you do or don't do that are self-sabotaging you and affecting your business. It's time to change your stinking thinking and turn things around by speaking positively, thinking positively, taking action, and doing the things that you need to do to get your business to grow.

Melanie Bonita

DAY 77

The Blame Game

STOP playing the Blame Game! STOP blaming other people for what you didn't do for your business or for your lack of success. It's time out for blaming other people for things that happened or didn't happen in your life or business. Or sometimes, you may even blame the wrong person. There may have been three or four people involved in the process, and just because it didn't work out for you, you blamed everybody in the process. They were not responsible for your project not coming to fruition. Take responsibility for your actions and do what YOU need to do in order to see your project manifest. Try seeking God's face to receive direction on what you need to do to make it happen.

Melanie Bonita

DAY 78

Decide to Delegate

In order to focus on producing what you need to in your business, you may need to employ other people to complete some of the day to day tasks. I know in the beginning when you're a solopreneur, you usually have to do everything yourself. But as your business grows, make it a priority to hire others to take on some of the other tasks. You want to be able to focus on income-producing activities and keeping the main thing the main thing. Hire a virtual assistant and delegate them to take on the administrative tasks. If you have an office outside of the home, hire someone to clean it. If there are any tasks taking you away from serving your clients, you should delegate them to someone else.

Melanie Bonita

DAY 79

I Never Thought I Had it in Me!

I was sure to work and retire from Corporate America. Little did I know, my husband had a plan of owning an ambulance company and it involved me. I was just being a supportive wife when I started helping out at our new company, Grace Ambulance Services. While my husband was busy working 16 hour shifts as an ER Nurse to meet payroll, I had quickly become the face of Grace. I used to be known as the boss's wife, now I am known as Boss Lady. I never thought I had it in me.

Mirabelle Tambe

DAY 80

It Takes Faith

God put you on earth for a purpose and has handpicked you to be a part of His master plan. Don't let fear keep you from the life God has planned for you. Faith without works is dead. You are going to work anyway, so exercise a little faith and let God lead your path to the life He designed just for you. Ten years later, and I am ready for anything. It just takes a little faith. Go for it; the world awaits your dream.

Mirabelle Tambe

DAY 81

Our Powerful Purpose

We accomplish indescribable successes when we honor our gifts and appreciate another's unique value. Connect with those who embrace and build you up with positive energy, then invest your surplus in others.

Say this prayer:

I am an heir of the highest King, equipped with God's divine power. I humbly give thanks to You for creating me with purpose to spiritually transform lives. I have the power over my destiny that is filled with supernatural greatness and favor. As I honor You by giving freely of myself, I am grateful for past, present, and future blessings so I can be an illumination of blessings to others. Amen!

Lady Keron R. Sadler

DAY 82

No Limits, No Boundaries

If you can dream it, you can achieve it

Since my childhood, I've dreamed of living my life to the fullest

I never let borders stop me from crossing them

Although we subconsciously build walls, I take on the challenge of breaking them down

An international black woman is doing more than flying

She is ascending to new heights

With the strength of a million strong mighty women —lifting as she soars

"I can do all things through Christ who strengthens me." Philippians 4:13 KJV

Makeba Clay

DAY 83

Prioritizing is the Key

"*But Seek ye first the Kingdom of God, and his righteousness; and all these things shall be added unto you.*" Matthew 6:33 (KJV)

Prioritizing is a fundamental key for successful businesses. Missed opportunities, broken relationships, and depression, amongst other things, is the result of not prioritizing.

If you're too busy for God, you, and your family, you're not walking in purpose.

Toy James

DAY 84

God. You. Family. Business. In that Order!

God – Spend time reading His word, praying and meditating. Isn't He the one who gave you the vision? Without Him in the process, failure is inevitable.

You – It's simple. Without you, nothing happens. Take care of your mind, body, and spirit. YOU need to be present.

Family – Timeless and precious memories are the result of time spent together, not neglect. The legacy you plan on leaving behind for your family begins with the memories you create today.

Business – Take care of your business and it will take care of you. Possess a spirit of integrity and excellence and you'll be rewarded greatly.

Toy James

DAY 85

Obstacles are Inevitable!

"*God is not a man, that he should lie; neither the son of man, that he should repent: hath he said and shall he not do it? Or hath he not spoken, and shall he not make it good?*" Numbers 23:19 (KVJ)

One of the most rewarding and liberating, yet challenging journeys in life, is that of pursuing business. Regardless of what stage of business you're in, you will encounter obstacles. Nevertheless, you must understand that obstacles are not designed to cause failure. They are just temporary growing pains. If you're experiencing setbacks, it's okay to seek help, take a break, or restructure your business. God gave you that dream because He equipped you to fulfill it. Believe in His promise. Obstacles are inevitable. Failure is optional.

Toy James

DAY 86

Favor With Negotiations

Start asking God for favor before you start making negotiations in your business. According to Psalms 5:12 (NIV), *"Surely, Lord, you bless the righteous; you surround them with your favor as with a shield."* That is a promise that He has made to us. So why go into any deals or negotiations on your own when you can go in with the favor of the Lord? That favor will get you so much further than time and labor. Think about the time, energy, and money you can literally save by asking God for favor in any situation. When you have favor in your business, you become UNSTOPPABLE!!!

Melanie Bonita

DAY 87

Put a Date On It

When you have a task to do, don't just put it on your to-do list. Give it a deadline and put a firm date on that deadline. When you put a date on it, it gives you a goal to work towards meeting the end result. When people tell me that they are writing a book, the first question I usually ask them is what is the release date? If you have a date, it can help push you towards that goal a lot faster than if you don't have a date. It's like playing a guessing game. Even if the date arrives and you didn't reach the goal, at least you have been working towards it. Then it's time to put a new date on it.

Melanie Bonita

DAY 88

Lean On The Lord

There may be times in your business where there might be some things that you just don't understand, but that's when it's time to lean on the Lord to get understanding. Often obstacles arise that are meant to derail or distract you. Have you ever been working on a deadline for a project and your computer or Internet stopped working? If you lean on the Lord and trust in Him, He will show you what to do during those times of uncertainty. In Proverbs 3:5 (NKJV) it says, *"Trust in the Lord with all your heart; and lean not unto your own understanding."*

Melanie Bonita

DAY 89

Daily Declaration for Women in Business

I am the BEST at what I do!

I work smart and NOT hard!

God is enlarging my territory!

I serve my clients with excellence!

The BEST opportunities find me!

I ALWAYS meet the RIGHT people!

My clients are chasing me down!

My creative juices are always flowing!

I take calculated risks in my business!

My income exceeds my expectations!

EVERYTHING I put my hands to prospers!

Melanie Bonita

DAY 90

Prayer for Women in Business

I pray that God would enlarge your territory and your business flourish. Wealth and riches are in your house as a result of you being diligent in your business. God continuously gives you new, witty ideas and inventions to increase your multiple streams of income. I pray that your impact, influence, and income increase because you follow God's plan for good success. You are always at the right place to get the best deals in your business. People are chasing you down to purchase your products and services. Because you operate in excellence and work diligently, you have an overflow of clients from referrals.

Melanie Bonita

Coming Soon

Daily Dose of Destiny
A 90 Day Journey to Discovering Your Destiny

Daily Dose of Discipline
A 90 Day Journey to Developing Order and Self-Control

Daily Dose of Victory for Veterans
A 90 Day Journey of Going from Tragedy to Triumph

Daily Dose of Holistic Health & Healing
A 90 Day Journey to Transforming Your Body from the Inside Out

Also By

Melanie Bonita

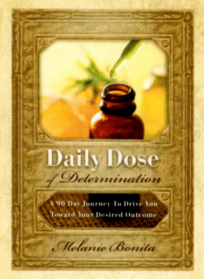

Daily Dose of Determination

978-0983546832

Paperback ~ $14.99

eBook ~ $4.97

Also By

Melanie Bonita

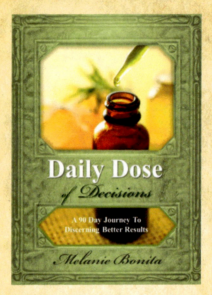

Daily Dose of Decisions

978-1467514132

Paperback ~ $14.99

eBook ~ $4.97

Also By

Melanie Bonita

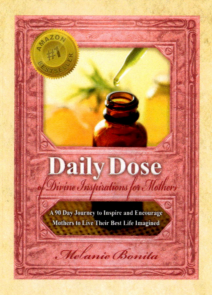

Daily Dose of Divine Inspirations for Mothers

978-1467514132

Paperback ~ $14.99

eBook ~ $4.97

Also By
Melanie Bonita

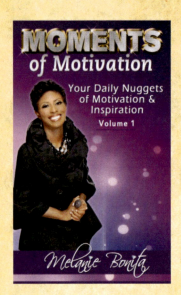

Moments of Motivation

978-1-4675-8270-4

Paperback ~ $14.99

eBook ~ $4.97

About the Author

Melanie Bonita is an anointed #1 Amazon Bestselling author, inspirational speaker, faith coach, prophetic dancer, gospel fitness instructor, poet, financial business consultant, veteran, and community leader.

At a very young age, Melanie Bonita was a very determined person who overcame many adversities in life. Although she had her daughter at age 16, was married at 18, separated at 19, and divorced by 20, Melanie obtained two degrees and purchased her first home by the age of 27. In 2001, she began experiencing various health issues; she was diagnosed with arthritis in both of her knees and was involved in three major car accidents which caused excruciating pain in her neck and back. Not understanding why the Lord would want her to continue dancing, Melanie began to realize that she was to no longer just dance, but minister through her body. Her life became a living testimony. Now, Melanie dances by the leading of the Holy Spirit. As she praises Him, she feels no pain. Her motto is "There is healing in your Praise." Melanie was also laid off from her job and experienced financial hardship. Yet, through all of these trials, she was still determined to reach her dreams. With the favor of the Lord, her tenacity and fortitude, Melanie now lives her dreams and is determined to help you live yours.

Creative Praise International was birthed in 2008 out of Melanie's obedience to the Holy Spirit. God has also given her the vision to help women live healthier, through dance and gospel fitness workouts. Melanie Bonita's Creative Praise International has been featured in the news, magazines, and on international television to include Newsweek Magazine, Yahoo News, CBS and NBC.

In August 2011, Melanie Bonita's book "Daily Dose of Determination" became a #1 Amazon Bestseller in the Kindle Hot New Releases in Christian Prayer Books category.

Melanie holds a Bachelor of Science from Bowie State University. She is a partner of Spirit of Faith Christian Center under the leadership of Pastor Michael A. and Dr. DeeDee Freeman.

She currently resides in Ormond Beach, FL and has one daughter, Crystal.

Connect with Melanie Bonita

Melanie Bonita
Ormond Beach, FL 32176
443-295-3673
ask@melaniebonita.com
www.melaniebonita.com

Like us on Facebook/
MelanieBSpeaks

Follow us on Instagram/
MelanieBSpeaks

Follow us on Twitter/
MelanieBSpeaks

Contributing Authors

If you would like to contact any of our contributing authors for information about their writing or would like to invite them to speak at your event, their contact information is included in this section.

Livi Anderson is an Instagram Expert, Social Media Speaker, and Published Author who has had great success in propelling businesses and individuals forward in marketing.
www.coachlivi.com

Evangelist Angie BEE is an entrepreneur, ministry leader, and author. She serves the Lord with gladness by leading #TheTOURthatAngieBEEpresents and her testimonial sermons leave audiences refreshed.
www.DaQueenBee.com
angiebeeproductions@gmail.com

Ayana Bernard, also known as "Yanni Ayana" is a radio personality, author, and speaker. She possesses great wisdom beyond her years. Visit her website at www.yanniayana.com

Dr. Evelyn "Doc" Bethune is an award winning author, a lecturer, and motivational speaker

working to expand the knowledge of Dr. Mary McLeod Behune.
www.marymcleodbethune1875.com
docbethune@tbginc.org

Bobette Brown is a champion for women, #1 Amazon Best-Selling Author, speaker, certified coach, and former U.S. Army 82nd Airborne Paratrooper.
info@ladybobette.com

Orjanette Bryant is a mother, wife, registered nurse, author, motivational speaker, and a business owner. Her books will change your life.
www.naturalnubian.net
orjanette@yahoo.com

Kelly Campbell is a Best Selling Author, National Speaker, and Master Coach with a gift for helping women who are hidden, be bold.
www.kellycampbellinc.com

Shonette Charles is the Amazon bestselling author of the novels, GAME ON and NAIL IT: Breaking into the Black Elite.
www.ShonetteCharles.com
shonette@shonettecharles.com

Dr. Shirley Clark is an International conference speaker, radio host, marketplace leader, and best-selling author of over 21 books. She's been

featured on TBN and more.
www.drshirleyclark.org
shirley@drshirleyclark.org

Makeba Clay is an award-winning thought leader on best practices in diversity, equity, and inclusion in the global workforce. She is an author, international speaker, trainer, and consultant.
www.makebaclay.com
info@makebaclay.com

Stacey L. Florio is a network marketer, and a physical health and financial advocate from Philadelphia, PA who was born on Mother's Day in 1966.
stayflo33@gmail.com

Jaclyn Gary is a wife, mother, and the owner of Mahogany Reads Café, an independently owned bookstore in Florida.
www.mahoganyreads.com

Toya Hamlett is the #TheVisibilityStrategist (Consultant, Graphics, Print Media, and more), #1 Best-Selling Author, Pageant Queen, Visionary, and Community Event Organizer at TDH Unlimited.
toyahamlettwinning@gmail.com

Odessa Hopkins, Owner, BizWomen Online, Co-Founder, Black Income Shifters.
odessa@odessahopkins.com

Tracy Horton is a Real Estate Investor, prayer warrior, encourager and minister of the gospel of Christ.
thorton5578@gmail.com

Toy James is the Founder & CEO of Inspirations for Women, Inc., Inspirations Gifts and Baskets, and is the Author/Visionary of the "Her Story His Glory" inspirational series.
www.inspirationsforwomen.org

Camille A. John is a Business Strategist and Financial Advocate. She's creating a legacy focused on financial wellness, business strategy, holistic health and philanthropy.
cjohnjenkins@gmail.com

Dr. Vikki Johnson has transformed the lives of over a half million women via her passion for Sacred Sisterhood through SOUL WEALTH!
www.vikkijohnson.com

Sylvia L. Johnson is a Biological Scientist turned entrepreneur and the Founder/CEO of

Johnsons Immediate Solutions LLC (aka JI-Solutions LLC).
ji-solutions.com
sjowens@ji-solutions.com

Tiffany Marshall is an energetic entrepreneur and mother of three amazing sons. She is the CEO and founder of HairMovement, LLP salons and signature haircare products.
hairmovement@ymail.com

Regina Nunnally is an Assistant Public Defender and Ordained Elder born in Daytona Beach, Florida. She attends Fellowship Church of Praise of Volusia County.
bbbjd02@gmail.com

Dr. Kelley Perry is a #1 Amazon Best-Selling Author, Business Consultant, Ordained Minister, Radio Host, and speaker dedicated to helping people turn their God-given dreams into reality!
www.kelley-perry.com
kelley@kelley-perry.com

Theresa R. Proctor, Transition Expert, National Speaker, and Author is gifted by God to Release, Revive and Realize Forward Movement in the lives of every audience she meets.
www.theresarproctor.com
info@theresarproctor.com

Reverend (Lady) Keron R. Sadler is a change agent of God helping people find and fulfill purpose applying her motto: *Excellence Without Excuses.*
www.LadyKeron.com
info@LadyKeron.com

Dawn E. Stephens is an INspirational speaker, writer, and coach. INspiring, Empowering and Equipping individuals and businesses to shINe from withIN.
www.DawnEStephens.com
@INspiredByDawnE

Kelli Y. Stonework is an anointed Presentation Skills coach, Aamzon Best-Selling author, Life Insurance educator, speaker, and community leader. She resides in Maryland with her husband and two sons.
kelli@kyssolutions.com

Mirabelle Tambe is the CEO of Grace Ambulance Services. LLC. graceambulance.com
mmtambe7@gmail.com

T. Lynn Tate is an Inspirational Speaker, Writer, and Blogger passionate about making a difference, and a positive impact in the lives that she encounters.
www.tlynntate.com
info@tlynntate.com

Lillie K. West is a Missionary, Speaker, #1 Best Selling Author, Travel Specialist, and President of Lights of Hope Foundation. She is the mother of Ricky (a Professional Choreographer).
www.about.me/LillieWest

Other Authors by

Fallen Chains
Samantha Campbell
ISBN ~ 978-0997992366

The Comback
Darrin Williams
ISBN ~ 978-0997992328

Early Morning Visitor
Rolinda Butler
ISBN ~ 978-0997992304

The Love Between
Tiffany Hayes
ISBN ~ 978-0997992342

Direction for Women in Business

She also rises while it is yet night, And provides food for her household, And a portion for her maidservants. She considers a field and buys it; From her profits she plants a vineyard.
PROVERBS 31:15–16 (NKJV)

Daily Dose of Direction for Women in Business–A 90 Day Journey to Direct and Guide Women in Business to Succeed will give you business tips to help you increase your impact, influence, and income! With impact, influence, and income, there's nothing that will be impossible for you! Come take this 90 day journey with us. It will truly direct and guide you to succeed!